If We Had Wings

THE TUSKEGEE AIRMEN
OF
WORLD WAR II

IN HONOR OF THE TU[...]
THEIR INSTRUCT[...]

⭐ **The Story of the Tuskegee Airmen** ⭐

By Mark Spann

Celebration Press
Pearson Learning Group

☆ CONTENTS ☆

═ ✪ CHAPTER 1 ✪ ═

Under Attack

On July 2, 1943, a young pilot named Charles Dryden landed his P-40 **fighter** plane at an American **air base** in Tunisia in North Africa. He had just fought a fierce "**dogfight**" with a German fighter high in the skies over Sicily and the Mediterranean Sea. It was Dryden's first actual battle with another plane, and he was lucky to have survived.

As he climbed out of the cockpit, a mechanic pointed to the left wing of Dryden's plane. A German pilot had shot a hole there the size of a grapefruit. Only then did Dryden realize just how lucky he was.

A pilot checks damage to his fighter plane.

Dryden was part of the 99th Pursuit Squadron, a unit of fighter planes. It later joined three other **squadrons** to form the 332nd Fighter Group. The members of the group were better known as the Tuskegee Airmen because they had been trained at an air base near the Tuskegee Institute, an African American college in Alabama. At that time the United States military was "**segregated**," which meant that whites and African Americans could not serve together in the same units.

The Tuskegee Airmen were the first African American military pilots. During World War II their most important job was to protect the American **bombers** from attack by enemy fighter planes. Bombers were large planes that carried crews of about 7 to 10 men. They could fly for long distances to drop their bomb loads. But at 37,000 pounds the slow, heavy bombers were easy targets for smaller, faster fighter planes, which carried only one man.

The Tuskegee Airmen later were also known as the "Red Tail Angels." Bomber pilots gave them this nickname because the airmen had painted the tails of their fighter planes bright red and because they had never allowed a bomber that they were escorting to be shot down by an enemy plane.

On the morning of July 2, 1943, Dryden and the other pilots in the 99th Squadron just wanted to fight for their country. It turned out to be a historic day for the Tuskegee Airmen. One of their pilots, Charles Hall, became the first African American pilot to shoot down an enemy aircraft that day. It was Hall's eighth mission.

For Charles Dryden it was not only a remarkable day in his career as a combat pilot but also the end of a long fight for the opportunity to serve his country in the armed forces. That was a different kind of battle, though, one that had begun several years earlier as he fought to become a pilot in the Army Air Corps.

Captain Charles Hall (right) earned the Distinguished Flying Cross during WWII.

CHAPTER 2

Learning to Fly

Charles Dryden grew up in New York City in the 1930s. Life was hard then for many people. The Great Depression had left millions of people without jobs and with little money. Adolf Hitler rose to power in Germany, which was building a huge army and threatening to invade its neighbors. It wanted land back that was taken from it in World War I.

But dreams were free, and Dryden's boyhood dreams were filled with airplanes. All he wanted to do when he grew up was to fly.

It was not easy for African Americans to learn to fly in the 1930s, however. Private lessons were expensive. There were also no laws to protect African Americans from **discrimination**. For that reason airline companies and airports could refuse to teach them to fly or to hire them as pilots if they did learn.

Even the United States Army did not train African Americans as pilots at that time. Whites and African Americans were not allowed to serve together in the same units, and the Army Air Corps, as the air force was called at that time, had no separate African American aircraft units.

Charles Dryden stands next to a Waco UPF-7, a plane used for training in the Civilian Pilot Training Program.

In 1938, Dryden started classes at the City College of New York, which provided a free education for New Yorkers. But the college did not offer flight training. He could not afford private lessons, and the army would not accept him for flight training because he was an African American. It seemed that Dryden would never get the chance to fly.

Then in 1939, believing that the United States needed to prepare for war, the government started a new program to train **civilian** pilots. These pilots could later serve in the military, if needed. This program, called the Civilian Pilot Training Program, would be open to all Americans.

Dryden eagerly enrolled in the new program, which began in 1940 at City College, and started his ground-school lessons. Flight training was at Roosevelt Field. Several months later he earned his private pilot's license.

Meanwhile, war had erupted in Europe in 1939 after Germany invaded Poland. By 1940, Germany controlled many countries including Austria, Czechoslovakia, Poland, Norway, Denmark, the Netherlands, Belgium, Luxembourg, and France. Great Britain was being attacked by German bombers, and many people expected the United States to enter the war soon to help Great Britain.

Dryden and other young African Americans completed advanced pilot training with the Civilian Pilot Training Program and tried to join the Army Air Corps. They hoped that the army would change its policy of not accepting African Americans as **aviation cadets**. However, the army still refused to accept African Americans for training as pilots.

Like other young African American men, Dryden was frustrated. He wanted the chance to fly the bigger, faster planes of the Army Air Corps. He was eager to serve his country, and eager to prove himself as a pilot. All he wanted was a chance.

Some members of the U.S. Congress were also upset that the Army Air Corps would not accept African Americans for flight training. In 1939, Congress passed a law directing that African Americans be accepted for flight training, but the law had long been ignored.

To make sure the law was carried out, President Franklin D. Roosevelt, as commander in chief of the armed forces, issued an order to the U.S. War Department in September 1940. The order directed the Army Air Corps to begin accepting African Americans in all departments.

Shortly afterward the Army Air Corps announced that it would begin training African Americans as pilots, mechanics, and other technical specialists. They all would serve in combat units separate from whites.

Dryden read the announcement on Saturday in his local newspaper, the *Bronx Home News*. The following Monday Dryden, like dozens of other young African American men, enlisted in the army and waited to hear from the Army Air Corps.

A group of African American men enlist in the Army Air Corps.

CHAPTER 3

Becoming a Tuskegee Airman

It would be a long wait for Dryden. In January 1941 the War Department announced the formation of the 99th Pursuit Squadron, the first African American flight unit. The first aviation cadets, all African Americans, were to be sent to Tuskegee, Alabama, near the Tuskegee Institute, for training. The ground crews would be trained at Chanute Field in Illinois and then later sent to Tuskegee. These men would be mechanics, cooks, weapons loaders, and medics and would do all of the work needed to keep the planes and the pilots flying.

In July 1941, after a ceremony at the Booker T. Washington monument on the Tuskegee Institute campus, the first cadet pilots began training at Tuskegee. Finally, in August 1941, Dryden received what he had been waiting for—orders from the Army Air Corps! He was to report immediately to the Army Air Corps Flying School in Tuskegee. He was finally on his way to becoming a Tuskegee Airman.

The training at Tuskegee was long and difficult. The cadets had to learn combat flying. Flying a large, powerful military plane at 300 or 400 miles per hour was very different from flying the little Piper Cub in which Dryden had first learned to fly. Not only were the planes that the cadets would fly at Tuskegee bigger and faster, they were also more complicated, with many new instruments and controls to understand. They also carried machine guns.

To fly in combat, the pilots had to learn special maneuvers called **acrobatic flying**. They learned to perform cartwheels and figure eights with their planes. The pilots had to learn to put the plane into a steep dive and then pull up out of it. They learned to fly upside down and to turn quickly to avoid enemy attacks.

The AT-6 was one of the planes used to train pilots at Tuskegee.

The Tuskegee pilots also spent many hours in the classroom, learning how their planes were put together and how to use the machine guns that each plane carried in its wings. The pilots studied the weather and learned Morse code, a set of long and short clicks that stand for letters and numbers. They used the code to send and receive messages with their radios.

They had to learn to read maps and to recognize places on the ground from hundreds of feet in the air. They also needed good math skills to figure out the correct course for their flights and make sure they had enough fuel to reach the target and return.

All through 1941, men arrived for training. The air base at Tuskegee also had some important visitors. Many people were curious about the men who would be the first African American military pilots.

One of the most important visitors to Tuskegee was First Lady Eleanor Roosevelt, the wife of President Franklin D. Roosevelt. Mrs. Roosevelt was greatly concerned about equal rights. She believed that all Americans should have the same opportunities no matter what ethnic group they belonged to. She traveled throughout the country, reporting on conditions to the President and encouraging people through the difficult times of the Depression.

At Tuskegee, Mrs. Roosevelt met Charles Anderson, who was in charge of the airfield. She knew that many people in the army and in the country still did not like the idea of African Americans training to be combat pilots. She wanted to show these people that the airmen were capable pilots and deserved their support.

Anderson asked the First Lady if she would like to go for a plane ride. She said she would. The **Secret Service** agents who protected Mrs. Roosevelt were shocked. They asked her not to go, and even called the President. Mr. Roosevelt told them that if the First Lady wanted to fly in a plane, there was nothing they could do to stop her!

Mrs. Roosevelt's flight was reported all over the country. It helped to convince people that the Tuskegee fliers deserved a chance to prove themselves in combat. Dryden and the other pilots of the 99th Squadron would soon get their chance.

Pilot Louis Jackson takes First Lady Eleanor Roosevelt for a plane ride.

CHAPTER 4

The United States Enters the War

Throughout 1941 the war in Europe grew worse. Yugoslavia and Greece fell to Germany, which a few weeks later invaded the Soviet Union. Great Britain was fighting hard but needed help. The United States continued to prepare for war.

Meanwhile Dryden and the other cadets continued to train for combat. More cadets were arriving at Tuskegee every month, eager to prepare for the likely fight against Hitler's war machine.

On December 7, 1941, Japan launched a surprise attack on the U.S. Navy Base at Pearl Harbor, Hawaii. Japan was part of the **Axis** powers, along with Germany and Italy. The Japanese had already invaded parts of China and other countries in Southeast Asia. They planned to take over more countries and islands in the Pacific Ocean. They were concerned that the United States would try to stop them. They attacked the navy base hoping to destroy so many ships that the United States would not be able to interfere with their plans.

Charles Dryden (second from left) is among those congratulated by Capt. Roy Morse upon graduation from the Tuskegee Army Flying School.

The next day the United States declared war on Japan. When Germany and Italy then declared war on the United States, the U.S. declared war on them, too. Dryden was at home in New York when Pearl Harbor was attacked. He was quickly ordered back to Tuskegee. With the country now officially at war, he would soon be flying in combat. Or would he?

On April 29, 1942, Dryden graduated from the Tuskegee Army Flying School and became an officer in the Army Air Corps. Afterward he and the other pilots from the 99th Squadron continued training throughout 1942. The war grew even worse in Europe and in the Pacific, but the Tuskegee pilots remained in the United States. The Army Air Corps resisted putting them into combat. Some generals still did not believe that African Americans could be good military pilots and serve bravely in combat.

But other government officials, including President Roosevelt, demanded that the Tuskegee pilots get the chance to join the fight in Europe. In April 1943, Dryden and the Tuskegee Airmen got the orders they had been waiting for. At last they would be going into battle! The 99th Squadron was sent to North Africa— first to Morocco and then to Cape Bon in Tunisia.

The 99th Squadron flew missions from Tunisia. Sometimes they were training missions. Often they were combat missions. The pilots would climb into their new P-40 fighter planes and escort the bombers across the Mediterranean Sea to hit enemy bases in Sicily and mainland Italy.

The 99th Squadron flew its first combat missions during WWII from Tunisia in North Africa to sites in Italy.

On the morning of July 2, 1943, the U.S. bombers headed for their targets on the island of Sicily. Dryden and the other pilots escorting them watched for enemy fighter planes. Suddenly they saw dust billowing on the ground below them. German fighters were taking off to attack the bombers.

Soon the sky was full of furious dogfights. Small groups of American and German fighters buzzed across the sky, firing their guns at each other.

A German plane attacked Dryden from behind. Dryden put his plane into a tight turn, trying to circle behind his attacker and return fire. His left wing was hit. Meanwhile the bombers dropped their bombs on the enemy targets and headed back for Tunisia, escorted by the Tuskegee Airmen.

Dryden was left behind. He fought hard but could not shoot down an attacking German plane. Another Tuskegee pilot came to his rescue, and the enemy pilot finally broke off his attack. The German fighter turned back toward Sicily. Dryden landed safely at the base in Tunisia—in spite of the hole in his wing— as did the bombers and the other pilots of the 99th Squadron.

The Tuskegee Airmen began to set a record that day. For the rest of the war, they would not lose one escorted bomber to enemy fighter planes.

Dryden's combat mission in July 1943 was just one of 1,578 missions carried out by the Tuskegee Airmen. They escorted bombers and attacked enemy positions in Sicily, Italy, and eastern Europe between 1943 and the end of the war in 1945.

Dryden was not credited with shooting down any enemy planes by himself, but during World War II, the Tuskegee Airmen shot down or damaged 136 enemy planes in the air and 273 enemy planes on the ground. They helped to capture the Italian island of Pantelleria in the Mediterranean Sea on June 11, 1943. It was the first time in history that a military target on the ground had surrendered because of air power. On June 25, 1944, Tuskegee pilots attacked and sank a German warship in the Adriatic Sea near Trieste, Italy.

The P-51 Mustang was the main fighter plane flown by the 332nd Fighter Group from 1944 until the end of the war.

Lieutenant Andrew Marshall, a Tuskegee pilot, was wounded over Greece.

Sixty-six Tuskegee Airmen lost their lives when their planes were shot down. Thirty-two of them were taken prisoner and spent long months in terrible conditions until the end of the war in 1945. They lived in German prisoner of war camps with little food. As the **Allies**—chiefly the United States, Great Britain, and the Soviet Union—captured more and more German territory, the Germans retreated. The prisoners were then moved in train boxcars to different camps. Often they slept on the ground. Charles Dryden was one of the lucky pilots who survived the war without injury.

When Germany surrendered on May 7, 1945, the war in Europe was over. May 8 was declared V-E (Victory in Europe) Day. Japan surrendered a few months later to end World War II.

Tuskegee Airmen served with several African American units. In 1944 the 99th joined three other squadrons of Tuskegee Airmen to make the 332nd Fighter Group. It was commanded by Benjamin O. Davis, Jr., who later became the first African American general in the U.S. Air Force.

About 450 Tuskegee Airmen flew in combat during the war. As a group they earned hundreds of medals for bravery, including an estimated 150 Distinguished Flying Crosses. Dryden and the other Tuskegee pilots returned home, proud of the service they had performed for their country. They hoped that the country they had fought for would now accept them as equals.

CHAPTER 5

After the War

Unfortunately things were not very different for African Americans at the end of the war. They had fought and many had died to defend freedom and equality. But once back home they were denied these same rights. The army was still segregated, as was much of the country. Like other African Americans, Charles Dryden still had to stay at separate hotels, eat at separate restaurants, and even use separate bathrooms and water fountains from white Americans in some parts of the country.

As part of the segregation in the armed forces, African American military officers were not allowed in officers' clubs on military bases. These clubs often had signs that said "Whites Only."

A movie theater for blacks in a segregated Mississippi town

In early 1944, African American officers of the newly formed 477th Bombardment Group had tried to enter the officers' club at Selfridge Field near Detroit and were turned away. When the group was moved to Kentucky, the officers tried to use the officers' club at Fort Knox and were again refused. After being moved yet again, in April 1945, just before the war ended in Europe, some of the officers from the group decided to challenge the "whites only" rule at Freeman Field in Seymour, Indiana. When they tried to enter the "whites only" officers' club, they were arrested. More than 100 of the Tuskegee Airmen were confined for 12 days.

After investigating, the Army Air Force ordered that the officers be released. All charges against them were dropped, except for three officers who had shoved their way into the club.

After this event and the end of World War II, many more people in the government and in the military supported the rights of African Americans in the armed forces. In 1948, President Harry S Truman issued an executive order. It said that there could be no more segregation in the armed forces. Whites and African Americans would serve their country side by side and share the same facilities. Dryden and other Tuskegee Airmen went on to serve in units that had both whites and African Americans.

In 1950 the United States went to war again, this time in Korea. North Korea had attacked South Korea, and the United States and many other countries fought to help South Korea. Dryden flew combat missions again during the Korean conflict, which lasted for three years. In 1953 the two Koreas signed a truce and agreed to stop fighting.

Many of the Tuskegee Airmen stayed in the U.S. Air Force, which had become a separate service in 1947. Some of them, like Dryden, fought in the Korean conflict beside whites. Dryden and other Tuskegee Airmen also flew combat missions during the Vietnam War in the 1960s and early 1970s.

Capt. Charles Dryden stands beside his plane on an airstrip in Korea in 1950.

Dryden served in the U.S. Air Force for 21 years. He retired as a lieutenant colonel and wrote a book about his experiences titled *A-Train: Memoirs of a Tuskegee Airman*.

Charles Dryden and his fellow Tuskegee Airmen were pioneers. They were early leaders in the struggle for civil rights for African Americans. Their bravery and skill as fighter pilots and technicians have been honored in books, films, paintings, and statues. The Tuskegee Airmen helped to earn the right for all African Americans to serve as equal citizens in the armed forces. They continue to be an inspiration for others as the struggle for true equality for everyone continues.

Lieutenant Colonel Charles Dryden (left) on his retirement from the U.S. Air Force in 1962
.